I Win

Rav   Finn   Tess   Asha

Written by Adam and Charlotte Guillain

The class went to the park.

Miss Lock got some sticks.

My stick is just a twig.
I will not win!

Talk about the story

Ask your child these questions:

1 Where did the children go?

2 What type of stick did Finn have?

3 Why did Asha's stick get stuck?

4 Why do you think Tess's twig won?

5 Would you like to race sticks like the children in the story?

6 What other games can you play at the park?

Can your child retell the story using their own words?